Metadata

A Basic Tutorial for Records Managers

ARMA
INTERNATIONAL®

An ARMA Standards Report
October 2009

Consulting Editor: Cynthia A. Hodgson
Original Composition: Cole Design & Production
Second Composition: ARMA International
Cover Art: ARMA International

ARMA International
11880 College Boulevard
Overland Park, Kansas 66210
913.341.3808

ISBN: 978-1-936654-97-0

A4918

CONTENTS

FOREWORD

This Standard is published by ARMA International as the leading authority on information, and is not registered with international standards bodies.

Comments on the content of this document should be sent to Editor, ARMA International, 11880 College Boulevard, Overland Park, Kansas 66210, standards@armaintl.org.

Rationale

This ARMA Standards Report provides a tutorial for the application of basic metadata elements necessary to support Records and Information Management (RIM) activities. This document focuses on current international standards and best practices guidance, namely ISO 15489, *Information and documentation – Records management*, and ISO 23081, *Information and documentation – Records management processes – Metadata for records*, and is organized according to the Metadata Conceptual Model set forth in ISO 23081. This ARMA Standards Report details how the information contained in these ISO publications—the international view—melds with the traditional records management lifecycle known to RIM professionals in North America—the North American view. This ARMA Standards Report does not include information about managing metadata elements as part of information technology system management.

ACKNOWLEDGMENTS

ARMA International gratefully acknowledges the generous contributions provided by the following individuals and groups, without whose time, effort, and expertise this publication would not have been possible. Company affiliations listed are those on record with ARMA International at the time of original printing.

Project Workgroup Leader:

Bernard Chester, CDIA+, ICP, IMERGE Consulting, Seattle, WA

Project Workgroup Members:

Susan Fitch Brown, CRM, NetSmith, Inc., Washington, DC

Glenn P. Gercken, CRM, Ungaretti & Harris, LLP, Chicago, IL

Mark Grysiuk, John Hancock Life Systems, Toronto, Ontario, Canada

Kelly Hamilton, Safeway, Phoenix, AZ

Babita Ramlal, PMP, Ontario Ministry of Finance, Toronto, Ontario, Canada

Douglas Schultz, Access Sciences Corporation, Houston, TX

Daniel Weathersby, Kroll Ontrack, Chicago, IL

Special Contributors:

Thank you to the ARMA International Standards Development Program's RIM Review Group members who graciously contributed to the vetting and review of this ARMA Standards Report.

ARMA International Headquarters Staff:

With appreciation, the following current and former staff members are recognized for their assistance: Nancy D. Barnes, Ph.D.; Vicki Wiler; and Kevin S. Joerling, CRM.

Purpose

This ARMA Standards report will encourage greater understanding and more widespread use of metadata elements. The records lifecycle is used as a tool to assist in this educational discussion of metadata. Although this publication is geared to a North American audience of Records and Information Management (RIM) professionals, it may be useful to readers in other geographic areas as well. Through the use of an elementary, field-based example, this ARMA Standards report illustrates metadata elements and their implementation in a records management setting where a computer-based tool is in place to allow electronic data management. It provides useful information for practitioners regarding metadata's relationship to RIM policy and procedure.

1 Definitions

Definitions for RIM terms in this ARMA Standards report can be found in the ARMA International *Glossary of Records and Information Management Terms*, 3rd edition.

2 The Importance of Metadata

The international standard ISO 15489, *Information and documentation – Records management*, defines metadata as "data describing the context, content and structure of records and their management through time." In ISO 23081, *Information and documentation – Records management processes – Metadata for records,* metadata is defined as "structured or semi-structured information, which enables creation, management and use of records through time and across domains." ARMA International, the North American-based authority on records and information management, offers this definition of metadata in its *Glossary of Records and Information Management Terms*, 3rd Edition: "structured information that describes, explains, locates, or otherwise makes it easier to retrieve, use, or manage an information resource." All three of the aforementioned definitions are similar, highlighting both the importance of the concept and the consistent manner in which it is regarded around the globe.

For the purposes of this ARMA Standards report, only RIM-related metadata will be addressed—that is, descriptive information associated with a specific content component of a record. This ARMA Standards report focuses on metadata applicable to records management processes during the stages of a record's existence. Typically, metadata exists apart from the content of the record. However, this distinction can become blurred; an example would be a record that contains metadata about other records. A helpful rule of thumb is that metadata is involved with managing information, but remains separate from the information itself.

Without proper metadata, a record may not be retrievable or may be improperly handled. Metadata also assists in maintaining the integrity and authenticity of records. The increasing use of electronic means to store records and information objects brings with it the need for more ways to identify records and information, including format, retrievability, and classification. Within the context of RIM practices, metadata plays an important role. RIM-related metadata aids in the facilitation and implementation of the organization's information processing activities and records management policies.

Metadata may be divided into groups based upon purpose. Many of the metadata elements are connected to the needs and processes of the business. A defined number of metadata elements will support records management processes. These metadata elements can be captured either through paper-based systems or within electronic systems, such as an organization's sales database or other electronic data repository.

3 The Records Lifecycle for Metadata

Metadata is important at every stage of the record's lifecycle. The international view and the North American view of a record's lifecycle have some differences as illustrated in Figure 1

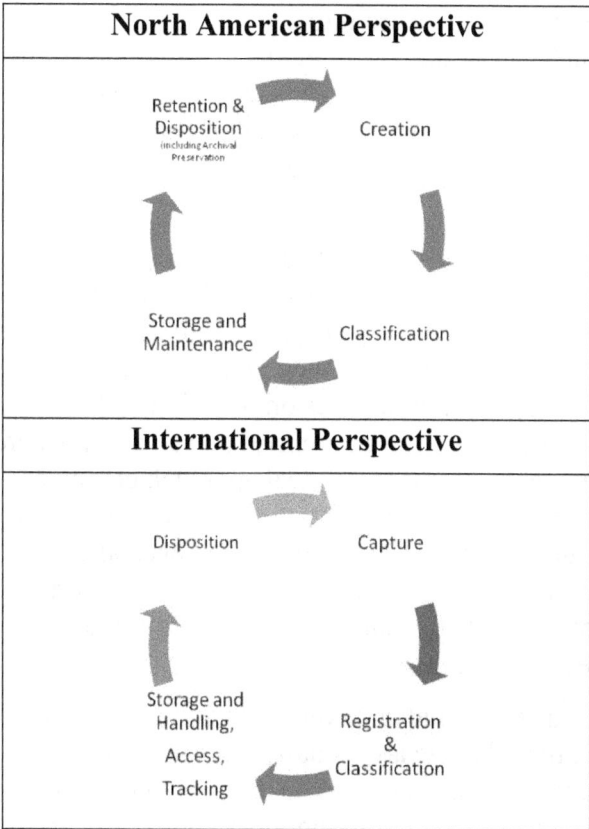

Figure 1: Two Perspectives on Records Lifecycle

ISO 15489 details the international view of the capture and registration of records. The North American view begins at the creation stage. A document may previously be created or can be created in the process of becoming a record. The concept of registration covers the moment of capture of the record into a system of classification, which can be an electronic database, an electronic document and records management system, or a paper filing cabinet. Both the international and North American views prescribe the need for classification.

The international view discusses storage, handling, access, and tracking. This coincides with the activities within the storage and maintenance stage of the North American view. Finally, the North American system focuses on retention and disposition, as well as archival preservation, where applicable. The international approach combines these concepts into disposition. Organizations must ensure that metadata are preserved even after records are properly dispositioned. It is important that metadata be maintained throughout the lifecycle of a record.

The international and North American views of the records lifecycle are actually quite similar. However, it is helpful to be mindful of existing differences when utilizing international guidance documents, such as ISO 15489 and ISO 23081, so that the most accurate and effective interpretation may be chosen for RIM-related business practices.

Records are created and used as instruments of the organization (active records). Ultimately, at some point in the lifecycle, they become inactive records. Inactive records may still need to be retained to assist in future decision-making or to meet external requirements. Inactive records can be moved to a less rapidly-accessed location such as a records center or an offline storage medium, without significant impact to the organization. Storage considerations and cost efficiencies are factors to be considered.

4   An Illustrative Example

To illustrate a RIM-related scenario containing metadata elements and their use, consider the example of a sale of a refrigerator. This sale, whether at a bricks-and-mortar store location or through a website, initiates several business activities. The primary record of the sale (i.e., the sales receipt) may exist in addition to other related records, such as a shipping invoice or a credit card receipt. Once the sale has been completed, the record of that transaction must be kept for a scheduled period of time in order to fulfill business process requirements. Record-related metadata may be added to reflect business and/or record lifecycle activities resulting from the sale. At some point, as determined by statute, regulation, and/or business policies, the record will likely become eligible for destruction.

From the merchant's perspective, a number of metadata elements may be collected at the time of the sale. Unique information may be generated, such as:

- Place of sale

- Name of purchaser

- Sales transaction record identification number

- Refrigerator brand

- Refrigerator model
- Refrigerator serial number

Informational items generated as a result of the sale, which may or may not be used as metadata elements, can include, among other data:

- Sales taxes
- Name of delivery vendor
- Delivery fees
- Delivery address
- Delivery date/time
- Salesperson name and/or identifying number

5 Metadata and Records Management

5.1 Capture

Capture is the process by which an information object becomes a record. This can happen when the document or information object is created. In the refrigerator example, a sales receipt will immediately become a record of the refrigerator sale. With other types of transactions, record capture can occur at a point in the future. For instance, a memo defining an organization's marketing strategies might not be captured as a record until the Chief Executive Officer signs the final draft. And that could occur many months after the original memo is crafted. Regardless of the format of the record (paper or electronic), capture involves content, context, and structure. It includes both registration (assigning a records identifier to the new record), and classification within the records system. Record capture implies that something has been created and needs to be retained in a way that will maintain its integrity and authenticity for a period of time spanning from the moment of capture to the endpoint of the record lifecycle.

Record capture implies that there may already be a set of existing series definitions into which the record may or may not fit. Record capture-related metadata choices may assign the record to an existing series, in which case the record will inherit the retention, disposition, and hold status of that series. However, after studying the business requirements and processes that created the record, the RIM professional may find it necessary to create a new records series and retention period for it. The series metadata will also assign a context for the record within the organizational structure and provide insight into the importance of that record in regards to organizational activities; its importance may take the form of legal, historical, or financial significance.

Each organization will determine the set of metadata that will be utilized according to its business requirements. As an example, the metadata for the sales receipt associated with the refrigerator sales transaction might include these items:

- Records identifier (sales transaction code)
- Document type (sales receipt)
- Product type (refrigerator)
- Retention (five (5) years or until expiration of warranty)
- Appliance make/model (brand/identifying code)
- File location (server or tape location)

5.2 Registration

Registration provides evidence that a record that has been captured, or created and captured. It may be appropriate to generate a unique identifier so the record can be easily located within the system. The registration process is a way of formalizing the capture or creation of a record and it becomes part of the audit trail. At a minimum, these registration-related metadata may be in place:

- A unique record identifier

- The date and time of record registration

- The title and/or description of the record

- The identity of the record's author, creator, sender, or recipient

The unique identifier can be part of an existing system or developed in accordance with organizational policy. Classification and registration are processes that can be linked, depending upon the classification scheme used and the complexity of the organization and its filing system.

ISO 15489 indicates that a record is registered when it is captured into the system; no further processes affecting the record can take place until registration is complete. Registration provides evidence that the record has been captured and formalizes the capture process. Capture can occur:

- at the point of creation of the record or information object;

- at a later time beyond the point of creation but when the record is still in active use; or

- at a time when the record is no longer actively used, but still has value to the organization.

In the case of the refrigerator sale, the record (sales receipt) may be registered when the transaction is complete and both seller and purchaser are in agreement that the sale has been consummated.

5.3 Classification

Classification metadata offers several benefits:

- It can be the difference between a search result being at the top or the bottom of a "hit" list, thereby impacting the speed with which an individual can find an object in a large collection.

- It can convey meaning that may otherwise not be clear by the object name or title alone.

Classification metadata has several implications within the broader topic of RIM taxonomies, as controlled language is important for identifying documents and records. If a retention schedule is organized by business functions and activities, classification metadata can be used to provide evidence of a business transaction by relating the record to the business function and/or activity that the metadata documents. It is usually better to organize by function, given that hierarchies can change due to organizational flux and retentions can change due to legal requirements. Classification of records includes assigning the record to a series of records with similar functions and/or retentions. Retention periods can be driven by the record type. In the previously mentioned example, the sales receipt metadata for the refrigerator sale may be classified by the manufacturer's model name for that particular appliance.

Security classification of a record may provide supplemental metadata elements. Classification metadata could be used to convey the security of an object, with selections such as confidential, internal intellectual property, and client intellectual property, to name a few. Classification metadata can be added at several points in the lifecycle; it will be added when a record is captured in order to associate the record with a file plan or retention schedule, and, eventually, it will drive the process of disposition.

5.4 Storage and Handling

While the international and North American views of storage and handling are similar, the North American RIM professional would usually refer to this stage of the lifecycle as storage and maintenance. While records are being maintained, they must be stored and cared for during the length of time specified in the retention classification. For RIM professionals, storage metadata may be more complex than other metadata, because the media type (physical or electronic) can affect the type of metadata that is required in recordkeeping. Different record formats have different storage needs—and this may affect how records are accessed. Each type of record should have an indication of its format for future reference. As an example, records may have barcodes that tie them to the metadata in a location system or file list. In the refrigerator sale scenario, the sales receipt may contain a barcode that links the record to an electronic database repository of similar sales transaction records.

One consideration regarding storage metadata that is universal across media types is whether the item is vital for business continuity. Records that are critical for business continuity purposes may need additional methods of protection and duplication to ensure that the record is accessible in the event of a disaster. For instance, an organization may require that copies or original versions of business-critical records are stored offsite to ensure access in the event that a major catastrophe strikes at the primary place of business and disallows records access.

Organizational policy defines the platforms to which storage metadata may be assigned. Infrequently accessed data may be placed on cheaper, less expensive storage platforms. Records with like retention periods and access frequency might be stored on similar media to ensure ease of access, as well as ease of disposition.

5.5 Access

ISO 15489 discusses access in the following context: "Organizations should have formal guidelines regulating who is permitted access to records and in what circumstances." In addition, "concerns around privacy, security, freedom of information and archives" come into discussion. In the records lifecycle, access occurs as part of the storage and maintenance of the record.

Within an organization, access concerns pertain to both internal and external users of records. RIM professionals ensure that records (encrypted or not) are available and releasable to the appropriate users. Access permissions are established and maintained as dictated by business function, requirement, and/or process. Access status for both records and users are kept up-to-date and assigned under the premise that each status is not static and is subject to change. Therefore, continual monitoring is required. Access control mechanisms are put in place to ensure that improper actions do not occur. Controls are needed because records may contain restricted information and should not be seen except by those with the proper authority. Also, it may be important to know who has accessed a record and when that access took place. There are many different approaches and technologies that may be used to implement access and security controls.

In the refrigerator sales example, metadata elements could provide assurance that sensitive or confidential information would not be accessed by unauthorized individuals. Each time the sales receipt data are viewed (electronically) on the company's computer network, several information items could be collected, including date, time, and user (viewer) identification. In this case, monitoring access and ensuring appropriate security controls for the record protects personal information and provides more effective RIM oversight.

5.6 Tracking

In ISO 15489, tracking concerns the movement and use of records within a system. The North American view of the records lifecycle assumes tracking activities occur as part of the storage and maintenance of the record. Many tasks are accomplished as a result of tracking, including: tracing the origin of a record after system migration has occurred, monitoring the movement of a record so a more complete audit trail may be possible, preventing the loss of records, and retrieving and/or identifying records when a specific action is required.

In the example of the refrigerator sale, the sales receipt could be tracked as it moved from the salesperson's computer at the point-of-sale location to the company's electronic data repository located on a remote server. Metadata elements track the record's journey, documenting a trail of activity that may include date, time, file path, server name, and user's identification number or code. With the potential for fewer lost or misplaced records, greater accountability becomes possible and overall efficiency is enhanced.

5.7 Disposition

Disposition occurs when the pre-determined time period has passed between the triggering event (capture) and the endpoint (date) as specified in the retention schedule. Once again, the international and North American views are quite similar, with the exception of the inclusion of archival preservation in the North American perspective on disposition. And, when records disposition occurs, the type of disposition (for instance, destruction by shredding or permanent preservation) would need to be captured as a metadata item.

In the example of the refrigerator sale, the triggering event may be the expiration of the product warranty period. When the sales receipt reaches its designated retention (e.g., the passage of the warranty expiration date), a review takes place to confirm that the business is under no legal or regulatory obligation to keep the sales receipt any longer. Once confirmed that there is no further obligation, the receipt should be destroyed by an approved method. Following destruction, although the content within the receipt no longer exists, an information audit trail about the destroyed receipt should remain. RIM professionals refer to this audit trail information as disposition metadata. At a minimum, it should include the following:

- Title/name of the file

- System identifier pointing to the system where the record originated (for audit purposes)

- Name of individual authorizing the destruction of records and if disposal services are contracted to a third-party service provider, the name of the vendor responsible for records disposition

- Records schedule identification or classification code

- Disposition date and destruction date

- Relevant comments or notes

6 Summary

Metadata elements are vital to proper records and information management. Practitioners are encouraged to understand and implement appropriate policy and procedure for the creation, utilization, and maintenance of metadata elements in their RIM programs. For further reading and to obtain more in-depth knowledge of the topics discussed in this ARMA Standards report, RIM professionals are urged to consult the ISO 15489 and ISO 23081 publications.

Bibliography

ARMA International. *Glossary of Records and Information Management Terms*, 3rd edition. Lenexa, KS: ARMA International, 2007. ISBN: 978-1-931786-37-9

International Organization for Standardization. *Information and documentation—Records management—Part 1: General*, ISO 15489-1:2001. Geneva, Switzerland: International Organization for Standardization, 2001.

———. *Information and documentation—Records management—Part 2: Guidelines*, ISO/TR 15489-2:2001. Geneva, Switzerland: International Organization for Standardization, 2001.

———. *Information and documentation—Records management processes—Metadata for records—Part 1: Principles*, ISO 23081-1:2006. Geneva, Switzerland: International Organization for Standardization, 2006.

———. *Information and documentation—Managing metadata for records—Part 2: Conceptual and implementation issues*, ISO 23081-2:2009. Geneva, Switzerland: International Organization for Standardization, 2009.

About ARMA International

ARMA International is the leading professional organization for persons in the expanding field of records and information management.

As of November 2009, ARMA has 11,000 members in the United States, Canada, and more than 20 countries around the world. Within the United States, Canada, Japan, Jamaica, Trinidad, and the European region, ARMA has 122 local chapters that provide networking and leadership opportunities through monthly meetings and special seminars.

The mission of ARMA International is to educate, advocate, and provide resources that enable professionals to manage information as a critical element of organizational operations and governance.

The ARMA International headquarters office is located in Overland Park, Kansas, in the Kansas City metropolitan area.

ARMA International
11880 College Blvd., Suite 450
Overland Park, KS 66210

800.422.2762 • 913.341.3808
Fax: 913.341.3742
headquarters@armaintl.org
www.arma.org